Money Management Skills

Understand Your Money with These 7 Tips!

Please Remember to leave a review on our book

Thank you from everyone at ACR Publishing

Table of Contents

Introduction

Many people believe that one reason the divorce rate is so high is that couples struggle with money. They can't seem to agree on a budget, spending, and many other factors associated with money. Lack of money is one of the biggest stresses in the lives of people. Around 50 years ago, couples could manage a family with one income. Today, couples can barely manage a family with two incomes. In fact, many people have two or more jobs just so they can pay bills and put food on the table.

It's no secret that people everywhere are struggling with money. College students are going to college, working at least one job, and barely making enough money to pay for school books and necessities. Many college students have to max out their student loan amounts so they can get money through their loans to help them survive during the semester.

People are often at a loss on how to manage their money for many reasons. First, they feel like they can't afford to save money, so they don't even think about it. Second, while they might have learned to budget a checkbook in high school, no-one really taught them how to budget money. Third, people don't pay attention to where their money goes. Of course, there are many other reasons that I could list but the reality is, everyone has a different situation with money which makes the reasons different for many people.

Are you at the point where you are so overwhelmed with money problems that you have started to lose hope in being able to open a savings account or invest money in other ways? Are you in need of a newer vehicle so you can continue to get to work but your credit is so bad you don't feel a bank would give you a loan? Are you confused about whether your credit is good or bad? Do you have so much debt you can't pay that you have debt collectors calling you several times a day?

If you're so stressed out about money and feel that you've lost all hope, continue reading this book. This book will not only help you understand money terms, loans, and different accounts, but it will help to take your new knowledge about understanding money and apply it so you can gain better money management skills.

Chapter 1: Understanding the Basics: Knowing the Language and Technical Jargon So You Don't Get Confused

Money isn't something we always think we need to learn. We've always known money existed and eventually learned that money doesn't grow on trees and you usually have to work in order to receive money. People know that you need money in order to pay the bills, such as rent, mortgage, car insurance, etc and people also know you need money so you can buy the things you need, such as clothing and food. People also know you need money in order to buy the things you want, such as a book or an iPad. Other than that, people don't tend to learn more about money, they just know you need money.

This is true - you do need money for nearly everything in life. However, there is a lot more to money than what the majority of people know. In fact, it seems that money has its own special language that most people don't know how to speak because no-one is around to really teach you money unless you look for someone to teach you. Well, let me teach you. This chapter will explain the money language that you're not sure you completely understand.

What is a Savings Account?

A savings account is a personal account you can open up at a bank. This account is where you deposit money that isn't for immediate use. For example, it's money you don't need right now to pay bills. While people open up savings accounts for different reasons, many people try to put money away in their savings account and not touch it for as long as possible. The more money you have in a savings account, the more money you will gain through the bank because banks will give you interest for having money in your savings account. Therefore, you can look at a savings account as an account which pays you interest.

You can also look at a savings account as a place where your money is stored for safekeeping. You're able to pull it out as soon as you need it, but until then, it's kept in a safe place, which is your bank. Of course, as history has proven with the Great Depression, banks aren't always the safest place to store your money. However, savings accounts are insured federally. This means that if your bank does fail, you will still receive your money from the federal government, up to $250,000 of it at least. This means that if you have more than $250,000, you're going to lose some of the money that was in your savings. But you're guaranteed to receive the $250,000.

The purpose of a savings account is to save up money for an emergency, vacation, or retirement. You can open more than one savings account and have them at separate banks or the same bank. You could even have different accounts for different reasons. For example, you could have a savings account for retirement and a savings account for emergencies.

Steps to Open a Savings Account

1. If you don't have a bank or credit union

you want to open a savings account at, you want to start by looking at what banks and credit unions are in your area. You can compare what they have to offer with a savings account. For example, what is the minimum account balance or what amount of money do you have to put into your savings account in order to open it?

2. Once you have selected your bank or credit union (make sure you can join if you decide on a credit union), you want to start gathering the documentation you will need to open up the savings account. If you're not sure about the documentation needed, give your selected bank or credit union a call and they can help you. However, you usually need your Social Security Number, Driver's License or State ID, and your mailing address.

3. Once you've gathered all your documentation, you can go ahead and open the account. Sometimes, you can open the account online but if you can't or don't want to go that route, call your selected bank or credit union and set up a time to meet with someone who can help you set up the account.

What Is a Checking Account?

A checking account is a bank account which you can deposit money into for immediate use. Like savings accounts, checking accounts work to keep your money secure. When you open a checking account, you often receive a book of checks, which is a method people use for paying bills and a debit card. The debit card works like a credit card except you have money in your account when you use it, so you don't have to worry about paying your bank back later. You pay for the items immediately. Both of these forms of payment is like having cash but you pay through your debit card or write a check.

Like savings accounts, you can obtain interest from the bank for your checking account, however, it's generally at a lower rate. Checking accounts can be used as often as you need. For example, you can write checks and use your debit card several times a day, you just want to make sure that you have enough money in your account to cover your costs. If you don't your bank will not only charge you an overdrawn or overdraft fee, which can vary from bank to bank, but they might also close your account. What happens when your check bounces will depend on your check's policies.

How Much Should You Save?

The amount of money you should make sure to save in your emergency savings account is anywhere from three to six months of your total living expenses. What this means is that you add up all your bills, grocery cost, cost of gas, and other necessities together to find your total living expenses. Of course, this amount is going to vary from person to person, but let's say that Fred is a single retired schoolteacher whose total living expenses every month is $2,678. This is the amount of money Fred needs every month to pay for his bills, medication, and all other necessities. Therefore, Fred should keep at least $8,034 to $16,068 in his savings account. If Fred is ever in an emergency situation where he has no type of incoming coming in, he could pay his bills and live comfortably for three to six months.

Unfortunately, for the majority of families, they aren't able to save up three to six months of their total living expenses. If you can't this is okay. Think of it this way, how much money do you need to help you out of an emergency situation? Of course, this all depends on the situation but if you have at least $500 - $700 saved up, you'll be in a lot better shape during an emergency situation than you would be if you didn't have any money saved up.

Therefore, the trick is to aim for a smaller amount, such as $500 - $700 and then do what you can so your savings continue to grow. Some people do this by putting a small percentage or dollar amount of their checks in their savings. Think of it this way - if you get paid twice a month, you get paid 24 times a year. If you decide to save $20 from each paycheck, you will save $480 each year plus interest. Once you start to feel that you could easily save more money out of each check, you start to save $40. In a year, you have saved a total of $960 plus interest. As you can see, even saving a small amount of money from each paycheck can help you build up your savings account.

Once you start to notice your personal or emergency savings account grow, you can look into opening up a new savings account for your retirement. When you do this, you could start putting money in both accounts. You could put an even $20 in each account or you could split the difference another way. Maybe you want to focus more on retirement than emergency savings, so you decide to put $40 into your retirement every paycheck and $20 into your savings. Every year, you start increasing that amount and soon you're savings accounts have grown to a larger amount than you ever saw possible.

High-Interest Savings Account vs a Checking Account

At this time, we will take a look at the difference between a high-interest savings account and a checking account. The biggest difference is checking accounts are more for daily use, such as depositing money and paying your bills. While some checking accounts might help you earn interest, it's very little if they do. On top of this, the majority of checking accounts don't allow you to earn interest. There are a few high-interest checking accounts, which are normally offered by credit unions. If you want to create an account where you earn money from interest, you're going to want to look at a savings account. But, you can't just look at any type of savings account. You want to find a high-interest or high-yield savings account.

With high-interest savings accounts, people normally see around 2% to 2.5% interest. The majority of savings accounts tend to have an interest of around 1.5%. If a savings account has less than 1.5% of interest, then you want to look for a different savings account. Try to find one that has a higher end interest plan. Because a savings account is meant as a place to store your money so you can gain interest, there is a limit to the amount you can withdraw within a month. There isn't a limit to what you can withdraw from a checking account. As long as you have the money to cover the checking account, you can withdraw as much as you want throughout the month.

A lot of people believe you need to have your checking and savings account located at the same bank or credit union. While there are benefits to this, you can pick different banks of credit unions to house your accounts. For example, credit unions sometimes have better interest rates for a savings account, people will open their savings account at a local credit union. They will then open their checking account at a different location for many reasons, such as not wanting to pay a monthly fee to keep their checking account open.

Today, generally all banks and credit unions offer online banking. This means that you can open a checking or savings account online, manage your accounts online, and even deposit money online. For example, many banks now allow you to take pictures of a signed check (front and back) and deposit the money this way. Some banks will allow you to do this for a savings or checking account deposit.

One downside to checking accounts is they often come with more fees than a savings account will. While the fees will often depend on the type of bank or credit union you're using, you might see ATM fees, monthly maintenance fee, a minimum balance required, minimum charge balance, and an overdraft fee. While savings accounts might have some fees, such as when you open up a savings account, they aren't as extensive as some checking accounts.

Both savings and checking accounts have different types of accounts you can look into. For checking accounts, there are free checking accounts, business checking, basic checking, joint checking, and minor checking. The most popular type of checking account is the free checking accounts, however, they are not always free. Many free checking accounts don't have a maintenance fee but they have many fees, such as a minimum charge balance or overdraft fee. Many married couples have a joint checking account, which means they are both signers on the account. Some banks will only allow minors under the age of 18 to have a student or minor checking account, which means one of the minor's parents also need to be a signer on the account.

There are many types of savings accounts, such as the online only, college, health savings account, and high-interest/yield. While I've already discussed the high interest/yield account, it's important to note that these types of savings accounts often have stricter limits than other savings accounts. The online-only savings account is pretty self-explanatory and doesn't always have high-interest rates. But you never know what type of interest rates you will find for savings accounts, so it's really important to look around before deciding on one. The college savings account is designed for college students who generally don't have much money, so they can't afford to save much money. However, a college savings account can help students in other ways, such as locking in their tuition and tax advantages. If you're often going to the doctor and have medical expenses, a health savings account is something you should look into. This account allows you to save money, generally out of your check, specifically for medical expenses which your health insurance won't cover.

Basic Mortgage Principles

If you are interested in purchasing a home, mortgage loans are generally the way to go. By the time people are starting to look at mortgage loans, they've been saving up for a house for years. While new mortgage loans come out all the time, they generally use the house as a backup, which means that the bank could foreclose your home if you don't make the monthly payments according to the mortgage agreement. All mortgage loans have at least one of the following:

• Fixed rate but with a variable payment (Graduated mortgages).

• Fixed interest rate and payment (Fixed rate mortgages).

• Variable rate and payment (Adjustable rate mortgages).

When you first start making your monthly mortgage payments, you're going to be paying more interest than principal, however, over time the interest payment will decrease and your mortgage payment will increase.

One of the ways you can help your finances with mortgages is to look for loans where the payments decrease over time. One of the most popular mortgages with decreasing payments is the adjustable rate mortgage. The payments fluctuate for this type of mortgage because of the loan's benchmark rate. If this rate decreases, the loan payment will decrease. However, if the rate increases, then the payment amount will increase.

Basic Retirement Savings Plan

One of the most important savings plans anyone can establish is a retirement savings plan. There are a variety of retirement savings plans you can choose from. Some of these plans might be offered through your employer, while other plans you might establish yourself. People often state the earlier you start saving for retirement the easier paying your bills will be during your retirement. Many people don't think of how their income will decrease after retirement. Unfortunately, a lot of retirees lose a large chunk of their income and end up needing to get a part-time job in order to meet their monthly bills. Therefore, it's important to establish a retirement savings plan or two for your security.

Types of Retirement Accounts

1. Health Savings Account – Because we've already discussed a health savings account, I'm just going to say one factor. You will never lose the money you put into a health savings account. Therefore, it's a good idea to establish one of these accounts as the older you get, the more you will go to the doctor and this account can help pay for medication and doctors' visits.

2. 401(k) or 403(b) – These types of retirement accounts are offered by employers. When you first filled out paperwork for your job, you probably filled out a form about one of these retirement plans. Both of these plans build through a percentage of each paycheck. Generally, people who work at nonprofits pay into 403(b) plans and people who work in for-profits pay into 401(k) plans.

3. Simplified Employee Pension IRA - This type of retirement account is popular for small business owners or those who are self-employed. These accounts are often chosen over 401(k) solo plans due to the

basics of setting them up and the amount you can pay in. The choice of the amount you can pay into the Simplified Employee Pension IRA is $56,000 or 25% of your income, whichever amount is smaller.

4. Solo 401(k) - This type of plan can be established by anyone who wishes to set one up. A person can contribute up to $56,000 a year if he or she is under 50 years old. If the person is over 50, then he or she can contribute up to $62,000 a year.

5. IRA - This is another popular type of retirement account. If you're over 50 years old, you can contribute up to $7,000 a year. For anyone who is under 50, you can contribute $6,000 a year.

6. Roth IRA - In this type of IRA, you contribute the funding after taxes, which means you won't be taxed when you deduct from this retirement account, as long as you're over 59 years old. You're also able to skip the mandatory withdrawals an IRA has once you reach the age of 70.

7. Simple IRA - This type of plan is popular amongst small business owners. In this

plan, employees and employers can match or unmatch what is put into the account with each paycheck. For example, both sides could contribute 25% or your employer could contribute less while you contribute more.

Guaranteed Investment/Interest Certificate (GIC)

A Guaranteed Investment or Interest Certificate is a return which will be paid to the investor after a period of fixed-rate payments. One of the most common types of GIC is a retirement plan as these are guaranteed payments. There are very little risks to these plans because of their guaranteed return. However, there have been cases where people have lost their money because the bank failed.

How Guaranteed Investment Certificates work is you open an account and deposit an amount of money. You can decide how long to leave your money in the account, with the length of time varying between a few months to around five years. Of course, the longer your money is held at the bank, the more interest you will gain.

While there are usually no fees attached to a Guaranteed Investment Certificate, you generally need more than $500 to open your account. When your term is over, the bank sends you the full amount.

Compound Interest vs Regular Interest

Regular or simple interest is calculated by the principal, which is the amount of the loan. Compound interest is calculated by both the accumulated interest and the principal amount of the loan. Out of the two types of interest, the most common type is compound interest, which people also view as interest on interest. What this means is each time you calculate the interest, you calculate it from your total sum. For example, you opened a compound interest account by depositing $5,000. Over the years, the total sum of your account is $5,500. When you go to calculate the compound interest, you take the $5,500 to get your new sum and not just your principal, which is $5,000. Regular interest would calculate the interest from the $5,000, no matter how much more you've acquired through interest.

When you look at Compound Interest, it can be calculated during any time of the year, however, the most popular times are once every year, quarterly, monthly, weekly, and daily.

Generally, regular interest is something that people understand easier than compound interest. Regular interest is what people get when they get a loan for a car or a mortgage. If people want to invest, then they will usually look for compound interest because they will be able to watch their money grow with compound interest faster than with regular interest.

Chapter 2: Borrowing Money

Today, it seems like people are borrowing money all the time. People borrow money from various businesses, friends, family, and by getting an advance on their paycheck. People borrow money for several reasons from needing a short term loan for an emergency situation to getting a mortgage or car loan. In a sense, even credit cards are like borrowing money.

There are good and bad ways to borrow money, which sometimes matters from people's personal preference. For example, some people refuse to take out a credit card while others refuse to go to a bank for any type of loan. Some people prefer credit unions while other people often try to seek help from relatives or friends before going to a bank or credit union to apply for a loan.

Before I start to talk about the different ways you can borrow money, I want to discuss some of the do's and don'ts of borrowing money. First, you do want to be sure that you can pay the person, bank, or credit union back. However you borrow the money, you want to make sure that you'll be able to afford the monthly payments associated with borrowing the money so you don't get yourself into more debt.

Second, you want to do some comparison shopping. While this won't be useful if you go to relatives or friends, if you're planning on getting a loan, you will want to compare interest rates. However, this isn't the only factor you will want to look at when searching for the best loan. You will also want to look at factors like penalties and any loan insurance you can pay a small fee for. For example, some banks and credit unions offer insurance for car loans where if you are injured at work and can't work for a period of time, the bank will forgive your car payments while you're out of work.

You don't want to be late on your payments. When you're late on your payments, you also need to pay a late payment fee. With that said, a good thing to look for when you're applying for a loan is a 10-day grace period. This is when you have 10 days after your loan's monthly due date to make the payment without any late fees. While this is not a habit to get into, it's a cushion if you ever run into an emergency. Sometimes you can even skip a month. There are some banks that will allow you to skip up to two payments throughout your loan's duration. As long as you contact the bank, they will generally just take that payment onto the end of the loan. Of course, if this is an option for you it's not something you want to aim to do unless you're absolutely in a crunch and have no other option.

You also want to make sure you stick to your budget and you seek help. You want to make sure you can afford the monthly payments before you sign your name on any loan. Generally, your loan advisor will help make sure you can afford the monthly payments as she or he will need to know how much money you make at your job, any other income you receive, and they can even discuss other factors with you to help make sure you can afford your payments. The banks and credit unions want to help you when you need it and many will work with you on a monthly payment you can afford.

How to Qualify for Financing, What Do the Banks Look For?

There are many factors that go into qualifying for a loan and banks tend to look at as many factors as possible to make sure they can help you with the loan. They don't just make sure you can afford the loan so they get their money, but they also want to help you advance. For example, if you go to a bank for a car loan, they want to help you get that car, but they need to make sure that they won't put you in any debt while trying to help you.

Credit Score

One of the first things a bank will look at when you're applying for your loan is your credit score. However, this isn't the only factor they will look at. If you know you have a bad credit score, you're going to be a higher risk for the bank, but this doesn't mean they won't continue the process. While they have their own rules and regulations they have to follow, they also know that people with poor credit scores are able to make monthly payments on loans, which will also help improve your credit score. So, if you have a bad credit score, don't worry too much. If you know the reason why your score is low, be honest with your financial advisor. Let him or her know what happened to decrease your credit score and ask if there is anything you can do to help increase it, especially if you're not approved for the loan. You can always get approved for the loan after you pay off some debt and raise your credit score. Lenders take note when you're trying to improve your credit score and they see this as a good sign.

Also, don't be worried if you don't have a credit score. While you will still be considered high risk and probably need a co-signer, you can still get the loan. The bank or credit union will want to help you build a good credit score, so you could still be approved as long as your co-signer is approved.

Your Income

Your income will be one of the first questions a lender asks. They will want to know how much money you make a month so they can help you find the best loan and amount for you. They also want to make sure that you have a regular income over an irregular income.

Payment History

Another factor your lender will look at when you apply for a loan is your payment history. If he or she sees that you've missed a lot of payments, you will be viewed as high risk. While this doesn't mean you won't get the loan, it's definitely a disadvantage to you. However, they will also take into account how many missed payments you have and why you missed those payments. This is when you want to be honest. If you lost a job and couldn't make your credit card payments for a couple of months, let your lender know. All these factors will be taken into account when he or she makes the ultimate decision on whether you're approved or not.

Debts and Other Expenses

While your lender won't need to know every single detail of your expenses, they will want a good idea of the expenses and other debts you have. Of course, much of your debt will be seen through your credit report. For example, if you have student loans and credit cards, your lender will be able to see this on your report. However, these reports are generally only updated every few months, so they might ask you to confirm your debts and where you are sitting with your debts at that moment. Again, it's important to be honest with your lender as he or she is trying to help you.

Traditional Ways to Borrow Money

There are a variety of ways to borrow money. Some ways have been around for decades while others are newer. There are some ways that financial advisors say you should stay away from and some ways that you trust more than others.

One of the more traditional ways to borrow money is through getting a loan at a bank or credit union. Loans have been around for centuries and are usually one of the safest ways to borrow money, providing you do your homework and get a loan the best way for you.

One of the most traditional ways to borrow money for students is through financial aid. While you can sometimes get grants through financial aid, you're almost guaranteed a loan if you qualify for financial aid. Generally, you can get around $20,000 in loans throughout the whole school year. Of course, this depends on many factors such as how much money your parents made the previous year, how much you made, and what year you're in at school (Freshman, Sophomore, etc).

Personal Guarantees vs Secured Loan vs Unsecured Loan

Personal Guarantees

A personal guarantee is basically a promise to pay. It's often established through a credit deal. Personal guarantees are popular among small business owners due to their interest in securing the business financially. Lenders will often ask the business owners who are signing the loan for a personal guarantee, which is normally the owner's assets so the lenders can reduce any risk associated with the loan. Therefore, if the business fails to pay the loan, the lender can go to the owner's personal assets.

Secured Loans

With secured loans, the lender will look at your payment history, credit score, and other factors when determining if you're suitable for a loan or not. On top of your promise to repay the loan, you'll also have to put up collateral, which your lender will receive if you don't repay the loan.

This makes the loan less risky for them because they assume you don't want to lose your property. Popular forms of collateral are vehicles, boats, RVs, homes, and land. The two most common types of secured loan are auto loans and mortgages.

Once you put up collateral, your property is placed on a lien. The bank or credit union holds this lien in place until your loan is paid in full. Whatever collateral you put up for the secured loan will be extremely valuable, in fact, it might be one of the most expensive items you own. This helps the bank or credit union ensure that you will repay the loan.

People who sign up for a secured loan aren't considered high risk because they've put up collateral. Therefore, your interest rate along with your monthly payments might be lower than unsecured loans.

Unsecured Loans

An unsecured loan is similar to a promise to pay. This type of loan is given by lenders after they've looked at your credit score, payment history, and you've signed the loan stating you will make the monthly payments every month. Other than this, the lender has no guarantee that you will make the payments and they didn't ask you to put up any assets to help make sure you pay.

People who sign up for unsecured loans will be considered a high risk, which means that their interest rate will be higher. This also means that their monthly payment might be higher as well.

New Ways to Borrow

Along with the traditional ways to borrow money, such as a loan through your bank, there are also new or more unusual ways to borrow money.

Paycheck Advance

While not every business is able or willing to give their employees a paycheck advance, some small businesses do. How this works is that business owners will either cut a check early, or they will give a small loan through an extra paycheck. Sometimes when you pay the amount back, you're able to pay the loan off through your paycheck. For example, you might make a $50 payment towards the company with every check until the loan is paid off. This will usually be shown right on your pay stub.

You should be careful with a paycheck advance because some businesses will charge fees for you to take an advance on your paycheck. If you chose to leave your job or are laid off for any reason, you might have to pay the full amount back before your last day on the job. Even if you've been at your job for years and trust your employers, you want to make sure you understand all the terms and conditions before accepting the paycheck advance.

Peer to Peer Lending and Its Risks

Peer to Peer Lending is online platforms which allow you to borrow money for a short period of time. For this type of lending, you go to these platforms and you borrow money from a person instead of a bank or credit union. Generally, the minimum amount is around $1,000. This type of loan isn't a quick loan to get as the application process takes some time. The lender will look at factors, just like a bank or credit union does, such as your credit score and payment history. If you're approved for the loan, it shows up in an account.

There are several risks for both parties on peer to peer lending platforms. Of course, one risk for the lender is that the person never pays his or her loan back. There is also a risk of fraud. Another risk is security. People all over the world are able to hack into internet sites and steal information. There is always a risk that your personal information can be stolen through the peer to peer lending site.

Line of Credit

A line of credit is a form of a loan that you can get from a bank. This type of loan, which some banks compare to credit cards, is a bank account. When you apply for this type of loan, you go through the same process you would for an auto loan or mortgage. Your lender will look at your credit history, payment history, and any other information he or she needs. If you're approved, you will get an account sent up through your bank account with the amount of money you were approved for, such as $5,000. You can use this $5,000 for almost anything but generally not as a downpayment for a house or a car. For example, you could use the $5,000 to pay off your credit cards.

The line of credit is approved for a period of time, such as five years. Every month, you pay an interest rate, which is dependant on the amount you owe on the line of credit. For example, if you've taken $3,000 to pay off your credit cards, you will pay a certain percentage of that $3,000 as interest every month plus any amount you want to pay until you've put the $5,000 back into your line of credit.

Your money in the line of credit will sit in your account until you need to use it. Some banks will attach it to your checking account so if you're ever overdrawn, the bank will automatically transfer an amount from your line of credit into your checking account and not charge you an overdrawn fee.

If your line of credit is not fully paid by the time your loan is up, then your bank might start to send you a monthly payment until you fully pay your line of credit back.

Personal Loans from People

Personal loans from people are one of the oldest forms of loans. These loans are generally nice because it's a form of verbal agreement between people. However, some people might have the borrower sign a piece of paper stating that he or she will pay the lender back. For example, the borrower and lender might agree to an I owe you.

Depending on the terms the borrower and lender discuss, the borrower might not have to make a monthly payment or have to worry about paying interest. People generally borrow from close friends, immediate family members, or other relatives.

While these loans are generally easy to manage and stress-free, they also come with their own risks. For example, if the borrower doesn't pay the lender back, this could damage the friendship between the borrower and the lender. A popular example of personal loans from people is parents lending money to their children.

Credit Cards: The Good, the Bad, and the Ugly

While many people don't view credit cards as a loan, this is exactly what they are. You are given a certain limit, similar to a line of credit from a bank, and you can charge whatever you want onto your credit card. On top of this, some credit cards will let you take out a cash advance. Then, you work on paying off the amount you borrowed from the credit card company every month. At the minimum, you have a minimum monthly payment, which is generally just a little above the interest rate you pay every month.

While many people don't see anything wrong with having one or two credit cards, usually stating they are for emergencies, it's possible to get in over your head really fast. For instance, sometimes the minimum payment is so cheap for people, such as $35 a month, that they feel they can take out another credit card with the same minimum payment. Some people tend to feel that credit cards are so helpful that when they max out one credit card, they apply and are approved for a different credit card. On top of this, credit card companies are notorious for getting people into situations where they take out too many credit cards. While it's always up to the individual, many people do not realize the high-interest rates credit cards have.

As long as you handle the credit cards right, you can gain a lot of benefits from them. Of course, the greatest benefit is being able to buy something one day and paying for it the next day. Many people state that the best way to handle a credit card is to pay it off every month. If you have a credit card and you're not able to pay it off every month, you might want to think about not using it until you're able to pay it off. This might save you a lot of money and stress later on.

Another tip to help handle credit card debt is to set your own limit. While the credit card company will give you a limit, such as $3,000, you are able to lower your limit. Try to keep your limit around $1,000 or a limit that you're sure you can pay back within a month or two.

Chapter 3: What Is Debt?

Is There a Good Debt? Can It Help You Build a Better Credit Score?

There is good debt in certain ways. For example, a college loan could be considered good debt because it's a debt which is helping you advance in your life. Another type of good debt is a house loan or mortgage because it's going to help you advance. However, the key to good debt is to know that you can afford it. While you can never be sure when you're in college if your higher education degree will lead you to a better paying job, you can be sure that it will advance you in your life in some ways.

Another good debt is debt that you can pay off every month, such as a credit card. You could also consider credit cards with low-interest good debt. Paying off your credit card balance every month is going to help improve your credit score as credit card companies will report you in good standing.

Another form of good debt is a loan where you can make the monthly payments on time, or even pay off the bank loan early. When you pay off a loan, your bank reports this, so it's listed on your credit report as paid off. This will help boost your credit score as well, as long as you made all your payments on time and in good standing with the bank.

What Is Bad Debt?

Bad debt is debt that you can't handle. For example, taking out too many credit cards is a form of bad debt. Let's imagine that you have five credit cards out and they are all maxed out, which means you can't use them. Because you only make enough to barely make the minimum payments on all your credit cards, this is what you do. However, you go through a couple of months where you're unable to make a couple of payments because an emergency came up. This is marked on your credit score and is negatively reflected. Now, you will not only have that negative mark on your credit report for seven years, but you've also caused a couple of your credit cards to go over the limit due to the late payment or no payment fees and then the over the limit fee your credit card company charged you.

Another form of bad debt is not paying your loan payments on time or your student loan payments on time. It's very dangerous to miss either of these as your bank might confiscate your collateral and your student loans could put you in default. Both of these items will reflect negatively on your credit score. On top of this, student loans can take other actions against you in order to get their money.

How to Pay Back Debt?

Of course, the best way to pay off debt is to have a job and stable income where you can live within your means while paying off the debt. Of course, people struggle from time to time and life events happen. When you run into a bad situation and start to have trouble paying a bill, see if you can borrow money from a family member or friend who won't make you pay them back right away. Another option is to call the company you owe money to and see what options they offer. For example, student loans offer many options, such as forbearance of a few months to a year. This means that you won't have to make any student loan payments for that amount of time.

Another way you can focus on paying off debt is to create a budget. In fact, if you haven't created a budget before, this would be the first step you would want to take when paying off debt. Another step is to pay your large debt off before any smaller debt. While people think it should be the other way around, paying your most expensive debt is often paying off your highest interest rates, such as credit cards. You also want to focus on paying more than your minimum payment on your credit cards. Of course, you can't often pay off your student loans quickly, but it might be a good idea to think about consolidating your student loans as this can lead you to a more manageable monthly payment.

Another great way you can use to pay off debt is with any extra cash you receive. This could be from work bonuses or an income tax return. Instead of spending this money on items you want but don't need, think about paying off your debt so you can start to focus on saving and sometimes spending money on items you want but don't need without racking up any debt.

Other ways to help pay off debt is to sell items you have that you no longer use or don't need. For example, how many children's clothes do you have your children don't wear anymore or what type of furniture do you have in storage? You can then use the money you make from selling your items towards your debt. Changing your spending habits and getting rid of credit cards and online store cards is another great way to manage your debt. The one thing you want to remember when you're paying off debt is that you don't cause yourself more debt. For example, don't try to pay down a bill by skipping a credit card payment. If you're going to pay more on a bill, make sure you can afford to pay more on that bill.

Debt Relief Grants

You always want to be careful about commercials on television or websites that say the government is offering debt relief grants because these are normally not what they are. While some nonprofits will have some type of relief grants to help you pay off some of your debt, especially debt that is attached to rent or utility bills, these aren't necessarily grants to help you pay off large credit card debt. These are usually in the form of debt consolidation.

With this said, there is a lot of government help

that people can get through various things, such as housing. For example, people who get help with their monthly rent through a county housing office will have a smaller amount of rent to pay out of pocket. While the company they rent from receives the right amount of rent, the county will often pay half or a little more than half of the individual's rent. This is often referred to as housing assistance. Other debt relief grants are thought of like food stamps, which is when the government gives family money so they can purchase food without bringing themselves further into debt. While these government grants don't take away the debt you owe, they do help you so you don't have to continuously build your debt, but you can start to pay off your debt little by little.

Debt Consolidation

If you can take part in debt consolidation for any part of your debt, you should invest in it. Debt consolidation is a great way to take a number of your bills and consolidate them into one monthly payment. There are different types of debt consolidation loans, so you will want to make sure you find the correct consolidation loan for your debt. For example, there are student loan debt consolidation loans and home equity loans. You can also take out a personal loan from some places to help pay off debt like credit cards.

Negotiating with Debt Collectors

If you're in debt, chances are you are ignoring phone calls from debt collectors because you feel like you don't have the money to pay the amount they're asking for. But here's a tip, you don't have to pay the amount they're asking for. Often, debt collectors will work with you to bring your debt down so you can make a number of payments and pay off your debts quicker.

If you have debt collectors calling you, don't be afraid to pick up that phone next time with these tips to help you negotiate your debt.

Make Sure It's Your Debt

Debt collectors can be as tricky as anyone else and they have ways to try to get more money out of you. Sometimes debt collectors have gone after people who have already paid their debt. Before you send debt collectors any amount of money, you want to make sure it's a debt that is yours and you haven't paid off yet. You can do this by asking them to send you verification, which they have to do within five business days. Once you are able to verify it's your debt, then you can call them to start making arrangements.

Figure Out What You Can Pay

Debt collectors will often work with you but you have to make sure they do. You need to go into the negotiation with the knowledge of how much you can pay them every month. And remember, don't give them your highest number first. For example, if you can pay them $120 a month, start at around $80 and chances are they will come back with an amount more than $80 but under $120. Don't become intimidated by debt collectors. They can't make you pay what you can't afford.

Know Your Rights

While the majority of debt collectors can be friendly and helpful, there are also several who can be rude and will try to push you around. You need to know your rights when it comes to negotiating with debt collectors. First of all, they can only call between 8:00 am and 9:00 pm. Second, they can't threaten to take legal action, especially if they can't or won't follow through with it. Third, they cannot harass you in any way. Fourth, they can't harass your family, employer, or friends for money. However, they can call them to gather information about you.

Stand Your Ground

No matter what the debt collector tells you, make sure you stand your ground and remain firm on what you can pay and what you can't pay.

Tell Them to Send the Agreement in Writing

You always want to make sure you protect yourself every step of the way when you're negotiating with a debt collector. This means that you request they send you the agreement in writing. This is in case you ever go to court for any reason or they've told you that you haven't created an agreement. It's also best to send them a check and not give them your debit card or checking account information. You want to make sure you can trace all your steps.

Filing for Bankruptcy

The first thing to note about filing for bankruptcy is to only file if you absolutely have to. But, before you even think of looking into bankruptcy, here is some important information to consider.

1. Bankruptcy will not eliminate all your debt. For example, if you have student loans, alimony, or child support, you won't be able to eliminate this debt by filing for bankruptcy.

2. There are fees to file bankruptcy. Other than fees, your credit score will take a huge negative impact.

3. There are different types of bankruptcy so make sure you look into the right type before you file. It's always a good thing to speak to a professional before you file for bankruptcy.

Chapter 4: New Ways to Manage Money

With the technology of today, there are many new ways to manage money. For example, you can download an app which can help you manage your money and budget. This will continue to change into the future as online tools continue to change and expand.

Online Tools

There are many online tools that you can use on the internet or by downloading an app on your phone, providing you have a smartphone.

Acorns is one of these great online tools.[1] Acorns is a tool where it will automatically round up your purchases to the nearest whole dollar. The change that you didn't spend is automatically saved for you. While this app is free for students,

---

[1] (O'Shea & Schwahn, 2019).

it will cost other people anywhere from $1 - $3 to download and use.

Mint is probably one of the more popular online tools to help you budget your money.[2] This app is free for people to download and use. You cannot only connect your bank information to this app, but it will also track your spending. On top of this, you will receive a weekly report from Mint, which will let you know how you sit financially.

YNAP is another popular app which will help you budget by your previous month's income.[3] While this app does carry a bit of a hefty price tag, a little over $80 for the year, it's a great app that will connect to your bank and help you learn how to manage your own budget.

If you need help in tracking and organizing your bills, then you should look at an app called Prism.[4] This app is great for anyone who has trouble keeping their bills organized due to a busy schedule. Not only will the app send your due date reminders for your bills, but you can also pay your bills through the app. On top of this, you can always pre-schedule your bills to be paid at a later date. If you wanted to, you could

[2] ibid.

[3] ibid.

[4] ibid.

schedule all your bills to be paid during one night each month. This app will also help you track your spending with your bills and help you create a budget.

Worksheets from Various Websites

Another form of online tool you can use to help your budget is through downloading worksheets. There are a number of worksheets through various websites that you can use.

Consumer.gov website is a site where you can build your own worksheet online.[5] This worksheet will start you off with the current month to see how much you spent. Through this, you will then create a budget for the following month.

Kiplinger is a website where you can use their online tool to create your own budget.[6] This budget is called a household budget and you use it to put in any bills and other household items you will need to buy throughout the month. You can also create a section for groceries and items

---

[5] ("Make a Budget - Worksheet", n.d.).

[6] ("Personal Finance News, Investing Advice, Business Forecasts-Kiplinger", n.d.).

your kids will need.

Work with Your Banker

Your banker is another great source to help you manage your money. Bankers know a lot about financing, balancing, and budgets. Many bankers, such as loan advisors, are financial advisors who can help you come up with solutions to your money problems or give you references for other people who could help you. There is nothing wrong with asking for help when you need it and your trusted banker is a great place to start if you don't know where else to turn.

Automated Withdraws to GIC Savings Account

When you have a Guaranteed Interest Certificate, you can withdraw funding from that account at any time, even before the maturity date. Of course, if you withdraw your money early, you will want to make sure you understand the terms and conditions as these can sometimes vary from place to place. You will also not be able to withdraw your whole Guaranteed Interest Certificate. For example, you might have to leave a minimum of $1,000 in your account, which would continue to gain interest.

Chapter 5: Live Within Your Means or Make More Money

One of the best things you can do in order to manage your money is to make enough money so you can live within your means. When you live within your means, you're able to pay all your bills on time, make at least the minimum payments on your bills, and have some money left over. While you might not have a lot of money left over every month, having a couple hundred dollars is better than having an empty checking account. However, if you are finding yourself scrapping for money at the end of the month or not having enough money to pay all of your bills, there are several things you can do to help you live within your means.

It Seems Basic, but People Don't Know How to Live Within Their Means

One of the biggest reasons people find themselves in debt is because they don't know

how to live within their means. People hear the phrase 'live within your means' over and over throughout their lives. But, what does it really mean to live within your means?

What it means is your take-home pay is equal or more than the money you need to pay your monthly bills, for groceries, gas, and other necessities. If you're not able to make your bills and pay for everything else you need on a monthly basis, you're not living within your means and you should take a step or two back and see what you can do to change your budget.

One reason people don't know how to live within their means is that they've never officially been taught. No-one has ever sat down with them and talked to them about creating a budget, or even figuring out what they bring home every month. For example, if your job pays you a salary, this salary isn't your actual take-home pay, it's the amount that you will put on your taxes as your income, but you've actually taken home less than your salary. Let's say your job hires you at a salary of $28,500. By the end of the year, you might only have brought home $20,000 because the other $8,500 went towards taxes, social security, and to pay for your portion of your benefits. This means that if you're the only income for your household, your bills and necessities for the month shouldn't exceed $20,000 to live within your means.

While people often take their larger bills into consideration, such as their rent, mortgage, or car payments, not everyone takes other bills into consideration. For instance, one of the biggest reasons people fall into debt is because of their monthly credit card payments. It's become so common for people to take out credit cards that most people have a few credit cards attached to their name. In fact, the average American has two to three credit cards. Each one of these credit cards has a monthly payment. Many people don't factor in their monthly payments with their budget because they feel the payments are too low. But think about it this way – if you have three credit cards out and each card has a minimum payment of $95, that's $285 total each month. If you're only bringing home $20,000 a year, you take home about $1,667 dollars a month. While this might seem doable, if you have to pay rent or a mortgage at $500 a month, you're already close to $1,000 and you haven't even factored in your utilities, car payments, car insurance, home insurance, gas, groceries, and any other necessities and bills during the month. Chances are you're not going to be able to live within your means if you have nearly $300 of credit card payments to make a month.

Another point to consider with only making your monthly payment on credit cards is that you don't save money doing this in the long run. Credit cards have interest rates and usually, these rates are pretty high, regarding your credit score. If you have a low credit score, which is bad in the mind of a credit card company, you're going to pay more towards your interest every month than your principal on your credit card. This means you will take longer to pay off your credit card.

If you're wondering how you can live within your means, here are a few steps people can take to make sure they're living within their means.

Know Your Take-Home Pay

You need to know how much you bring home from your paychecks. You can do this by averaging your paychecks. Generally, if you make around the same every month, you're going to notice an average amount that's taken out of your salary for taxes. For example, if you make $1,000 every two weeks, you're going to realize that around $120 is taken out for taxes and social security. This means your take-home pay per paycheck is $880. If you get paid twice a month, you receive about $1,760. However, if you get paid bi-weekly, you're going to make more throughout the year, and a couple of months out of the year, your take-home income will be $880 more than your regular months.

Increase Your Income

For most people, even people who live alone, $1,760 a month isn't a lot of money as sometimes rent is close to around $600. While it's doable for many people who live alone, it's still generally pretty close to what they have to make for bills and can leave them in a bind if there is ever an emergency. This is one reason so many people have more than one job, in order to increase their income so they can live comfortably and be able to save for an emergency situation. There are many ways to increase your income. For example, you could request a raise. However, because many jobs are unable to give a raise at your request, you can also see if overtime is available for your job. Even if you work a few hours a week more, the money will add up quickly and you should have been luck at making your bills and having a little more money left over.

Spend Less Money Than You Take Home

If you can't or don't want to take the time to get a second job, you will just need to re-adjust your income so you spend less money than you bring home. There are many ways to do this, such as looking to see what your cable or internet bill is, cell phone bill, and other bills. You could even look at moving to a cheaper apartment or getting a roommate. Maybe you would be able to make changes within your grocery bill or other products you buy, such as shampoos. Sometimes even changing stores is a great way to save money. For example, half-priced or dollar stores offer things like soaps, shampoos, and groceries which are just as good as any other store.

Start an Emergency Fund

You don't need to save a lot of money to start up an emergency fund. You can simply open a savings account at a bank and start saving $20-$40 out of each one of your checks. All you need to do is work on your budget so you know what you can afford to save each paycheck. This will help you if you ever run into an emergency situation. This way, you will be less likely to need to look for a short-term loan or borrow money from someone else you need to pay back.

Don't Try to be Like Someone Else

Sometimes people find themselves struggling to make bills or going into debt because they are trying to keep up with their neighbors or friends. You need to worry about yourself and your own income and bills. As long as you can live within your means, this is all you have to worry about. You never know, the Jones' could be falling into debt themselves!

Stay Away From Credit Cards

Many people believe one of the smartest things you can to do manage your money is to stay away from credit cards. Not only is this because of the monthly minimum payments which often cause you to get into a bigger hole financially than anything else but because they can be too tempting for many people. It's nice to be able to go out and buy what we want and need when we can, which is what people often use credit cards for, but it's more important to be able to manage your money within your means. When you use credit cards, you're not living within your means. Even if you can make the minimum payment, you're purchasing items which you can't afford at the moment. This isn't living within your means. On top of this, credit card companies can often change terms at any given moment, close your account, or decrease your credit limit. All of these situations can harm your credit score.

Save For Your Purchase

Instead of using credit cards for purchases you can't make at the moment, start saving up for them. Think about it – if your credit card limit is $1,000, it won't take you very long to save up for what you want instead of using a credit card and then paying that $1,000 back plus interest. In the end, saving up so you can make your big purchase is going to save you money and help you manage your budget over getting a credit card or another line of credit.

If you're still not sure about how to live within your means, or wondering how you're doing now, here are some warning signs which will tell you that you're not living within your means.

You're Not Saving Enough

Not being able to save even 5% of your take-home pay is often a good warning sign that you're not living within your means. As a general rule, people should strive to save about 10% to 20% of their monthly take-home pay. But even when you're paying off debt, it's important to save and make sure you can put at least 5% into your savings. If you can't you're outside of your means and you should adjust your budget or try to increase your take-home pay.

You're Fearful When You Spend Money

Another warning sign that you're not living within your means is that you're always afraid of running out of money, even when you're making smaller purchases. You're always worried that you didn't budget correct and, therefore, won't be able to have enough money to make a bill or two you need to make.

Your Credit Card Always Has a Balance

Even if you have only one or two credit cards, you're never able to fully pay off the balance. This happens because you need to use the card to help you buy groceries or you just can't afford to pay off the balance.

You Don't Have Money Left Over

There is a popular saying that most people in America live paycheck to paycheck. However, you're living outside of your means when the money from your paycheck doesn't last until your next paycheck. In this case, you often find yourself with little to no money (or worse in debt) to your bank.

You Pay Your Bank Overdraft Fees

You know you're living beyond your means when you regularly pay your bank overdraft fees because you wrote a check and don't have money in your account to cover that check. Banks generally charge anywhere from $30 to $50 per overdrawn check. While they might hold the check for a while in your account, this fee you need to pay on top of any money you went over in your account. For example, if you had $300 in your account and your bank received a $500 check, you now owe your bank $200 plus the overdraft fee.

If You Don't Know How to Budget, Your Debt Will Get out of Control

One of the best ways to live within your means is to make sure you have a budget that you can afford and stick to it. Many people who live beyond their means don't make a budget because they don't think there is a point as they never have any money left over at the end of the month. However, if you establish a budget which allows you to live within your means, you will be able to take control of your debt. People who don't know how to budget often let their debt get out of control.

Another reason it's important to create a budget and live within your means is so you stay away from the lifestyle you can't afford. It's often hard to change your spending habits so you can afford your lifestyle. Therefore, it's best to keep your budget under your take-home pay.

If you've realized your debt is out of control, you can take a look at the following tips when trying to get your debt under control.

Make Minimum Payments On Time

Sometimes people feel they can skip a bill one month if they pay it later or the next month. This is often the case with credit cards and is a bad habit to fall into. One of the biggest reasons you don't want to do this is because the credit card company will charge you a missed payment or late payment fee. This fee is often in the range of $35 - $55 and can send you over your limit if you're close to your limit. When this happens, your credit card company will also charge you an 'over the limit' fee. On top of making minimum payments on time, it's always a good idea to pay a little above your minimum payment. For example, if your minimum payment is $35, you might want to pay $40-$45. This will help increase the amount of money which goes towards your principal as most of your minimum payment balance goes towards interest on your credit card.

Pay Off Your Credit Cards

If you have any credit cards, one of the first things you should do to save yourself money is to pay off your credit cards. This will give you the amount of money you have to spend on the minimum payment of these credit cards, which you could work into putting towards savings. Often, if you call the credit card company they will work with you on this. Some credit card companies will take off any fees you've racked up over the last couple months or so if you pay them a large amount. Even if you can't pay off your credit cards in a month, try to pay them off over a period of time.

Earn Extra Income

You could always try picking up a second job in order to help yourself pay off some of your debt. Even if you feel like you won't be able to handle two jobs very long, you can use the income from your second job to pay off your debt. Depending on how much debt you have, you might be able to pay it off within a few months. Another way you can earn extra income is by holding a garage sale or selling items you no longer use. If you have a storage shed, this is a great place to start. See what items you can clean up to sell. A great time to do this is during community-wide rummage sales. Most communities hold a sale like this in the spring or fall. Anyone from the community can sign up to take part in a community-wide rummage sale. If you're interested in selling items, this would be a great way to start as these type of rummage sales are widely publicized in your area. Because they are advertised, they often bring more people into your community who are ready and willing to find good deals in the rummage sales.

Chapter 6: Mentally Changing the Way You Think of Managing Wealth

Sometimes, the reason we have trouble living within our means is because of the ways we think about money. For example, if you grew up where your parents paid for everything because they could afford to, you might have a tough time living on your own income. You may have also grown up poor, so you were never allowed to have many luxuries in life. Then, you started to feel you were really making money when you received a new job and now you've found that you don't know how to budget correctly because you feel you're making way more money than you know what to do with. In order to change the way we manage our money, we need to mentally change the way we think about our money.

Changing the Ways You Think About Money

If you need to work on changing the way you think about money, here are a few tips to help you along in this process.

Money is Tool, Not a Result

People often think that money is the result they receive for their hard work. However, if you change this mindset and start seeing money as a tool instead of a result, you're more likely to make better decisions over your finances. For example, you have a couple of thousand dollars stashed away in a desk drawer. You're out shopping when you notice the newer televisions are on sale for a little over $2,000. You know that, even with tax, you would be able to afford this because of the money you have in your desk drawer. Someone who sees money, as a result, will justify purchasing the television with this money because they've earned it for their hard work. But, someone who sees money as a tool is going to think they could put that $2,000 into a high-interest savings account and start collecting interest off the $2,000.

Money and Emotions Shouldn't Mix

Another way to help you think more positively and healthily about money is to not place money on an emotional ladder. There is nothing emotional about money. However, for people who struggle to get by on their income or who grew up poor, they often see money as a sign of stress. But, if you budget correctly, there will be nothing stressful about money. You have to keep the emotions away from your money. Furthermore, in order to be able to see money as a tool, a way you can invest to make more money, you're going to have to let go of your emotions.

Pay Yourself First

Some people get so caught up in thinking they have to pay off all their debt as quickly as possible in order to start saving money. This is not true. While you want to focus on paying off your debt, you want to make sure you're taken care of first. Therefore, one of the biggest pieces of advice wealthy people will tell you is to pay yourself first and then worry about your debt. Basically, wealthy people will tell you the most important thing you can do is secure your financial future and the debt will decrease as time goes on.

Money: The Way Your Parents Think About Money and the New Way to Manage It

Every generation will think differently about money. Perhaps the way our parents thought about money and taught us how to save money isn't the best way to manage money anymore. For example, many parents might have just put their money into a savings account. However, you might find better ways to gain interest by saving money into different accounts, such as a CD. Just because your parents taught you to think about money one way doesn't mean it's the right way for you. You need to find the best way to manage your money. This might be through a budget, which is something your parents never did or taught you.

Chapter 7: What to Do with Small Savings to Make It Work for You

Saving It Under Your Pillow Doesn't Work Anymore

Many people, especially those who lived through the Great Depression, felt that banks were not the safest place for their money. Therefore, people started to save money in various places throughout their house, whether it was a location in their desk or safe. However, with the increase in inflation and many other ways to save money, keeping money tucked away in your home isn't the best option anymore.

Other than the fact that you can gain interest in a savings account, CDs, and other methods, it's a lot easier to spend the money if it's available by opening a drawer. We are living in a different time than our parents and our grandparents. Not only do more people lack the self-discipline to not touch money when it's available to them, but we don't think of money in the same way. Generally, people don't understand the value of a dollar like the older generations did.

Join a Peer to Peer Lending Group

If you don't have a large amount of money and very little savings, one way to help increase your wealth is by joining a peer to peer lending group. There are dozens of these types of groups online. This type of group, which we've talked a bit about previously, is full of people who are in need of money and people who want to invest their money.

Instead of going to a bank, you go to another individual who wants to help you out or you set up an account so you can help someone else out. Today, this is one of the most popular ways to loan money and it's growing at a quick rate. In fact, one study noticed a 110% increase in peer to peer lending in 2006.[7] Since then, it's only

---

[7] (Muller, 2018).

continued to grow.

One of the best peer to peer lending sights online is known as Prosper.[8] Prosper was the first peer to peer site established and now has over 700,000 members. This website will allow you to borrow up to $40,000 and pay it back within three to five years.

Lending Club is another peer to peer lending sight and, while it's very similar to Prosper, it started in 2007, two years after Prosper.[9] This site has about four different loans to choose from. For example, you can get an auto refinancing loan, business loan, personal loan, or patient loan. A patient loan is a loan that you can use to help pay for medical expenses.

Invest in a Small Business

Small businesses are becoming more popular as time goes on and part of the reason is that people can gain a lot of money when they invest in a small business. While it always seems to be a bit of a risk at first, small businesses can grow

---

[8] Ibid.

[9] ibid.

quickly, which helps make the people who invest in them rather wealthy in a small amount of time. For example, a couple might invest in starting up a real estate business. At first, they get a loan to help them purchase their first multi-family building. After they establish themselves with this building, everyone is paying rent, the bills for the building are being paid, and they've saved up money, they decide to purchase another building. Over time, their buildings and investments in their company have grown.

Penny Stock Trading

Penny stocks are stocks that people highly question before they buy into them because they are only valued at under $1, however, sometimes the stocks are valued at under $5. The way you're going to make money when you invest in penny stocks is by picking the right stocks to invest. For example, you want to invest in the stocks that seem to have a good history over the stocks that seem to struggle. One of the biggest things about investing and trading in the stock market, is you want to make sure you understand the basics and look for stocks which are known to have a strong reputation.

If you get involved with penny stocks, there are some things you want to pay attention to. First, you want to know why the stocks are at the price they are at. For instance, if you're looking for a stock to invest in and you notice one that is sitting well, you want to dig to see if you can find out why. The reasons for this is there are a lot of people who invest in penny stocks as they see the price inflate, which means that it's a good stock to invest in. However, what these people didn't know is that this stock was involved in a fraud. Some people purchase penny stocks so they will inflate the price, which makes other people purchase the stocks. Then, when they see the price has inflated to a certain point, they all sell and they are left with a huge profit. However, the other investors who didn't understand what was happening have now lost money. This is called the Pump and Dump scheme.

Another popular scheme you want to watch out for with penny stocks is called the Guru scheme. This scheme often starts off as some type of advertisement someone places to let people know that they became rich by taking these steps as a penny stock investor. The problem is, the person never became rich through those steps. These Gurus often state that in order to find out their secrets, you have to pay them a low sum and join in on their website or class they are holding.

Make Money Even with Small Amounts of Money

There are a variety of ways you can watch your wealth grow even with very little money. Many people think that they have to save a certain amount of money in order to invest or have a certain amount before they can make money. This isn't true. In fact, you can start investing money into stocks when you only have a few hundred dollars. The only thing is you will want to make sure you understand the stock business. You can also invest a few thousand dollars into a savings account or a CD. While we won't be able to discuss all the ways in this section of the book, we will take time to discuss a few.

Stocks

Of course, you're going to want to do your own research before you start investing in stocks, but they are a great way to watch your wealth grow, providing you do it correctly. There are a large number of stocks you can invest in and with a tool known as the Robo Advisor, investing in stocks has become easier and less work for you. While people say you don't need any prior stock investing experience if you use a Robo Advisor, it's still a good idea to understand the basics of the stock market.

Cookie Jar

The cookie jar savings is still a good option, providing you have the self-discipline to leave the money alone until you can safely place it in a savings account where it can grow with interest. A cookie jar savings is similar to a piggy bank, but you can often hold more money in the cookie jar, especially if you get a larger cookie jar. However, you want to watch out because it's also easier to take money out of the cookie jar. You should also make sure that whenever your cookie jar is full, you bring it into the bank and deposit it into a high-interest savings account. This will help your small amount of money grow into a large sum.

The $1 Approach

This approach is similar to the cookie jar approach, and you're going to need self-discipline in order to handle this approach. Basically, you focus on saving all your dollar bills. You can save them in an envelop or type of piggy bank. The trick is you don't want to touch these and when you feel like you have enough dollar bills, you want to make sure you place them in some type of savings account, whether it's your emergency fund, retirement fund, or a regular high-interest savings account. If you use cash a lot when you're shopping, you will find that your $1 bills add up quickly, which will mean your savings add up quickly. Of course, the major key is not to spend this money, which can be hard when you're short on money for the month. However, it's also important to remember to pay yourself first and start up a savings account or two as you need to invest in your financial future along with paying your bills. You could also use this approach with pennies, however, it'll take you longer to build up your savings with pennies than with $1. Or you could do both. Really, it's up to you but if you have the self-discipline to use an approach like this, it's well worth the shot!

Other Forms of Savings Accounts

There are a variety of other types of savings accounts which will allow you to place a small amount of money in them and watch your wealth grow. For example, you could invest money in CDs or bonds, such as savings bonds. The trick is to do your research so you know what is the best type of investment for you. You also want to make sure you understand the basics of the savings account you're looking into and note any maturity dates. For example, savings bonds often have maturity dates of a few years. However, they also collect interest, so they are a great way to save some money for your future.

Above all, no matter how you decide to invest your small amount of money, you want to make sure you follow your budget and you can pay your bills and live within your means without needing this small amount of money. You also want to make sure you pick the right investment plan for you. For example, you don't want to invest in the stock market and then realize you have no idea what you're doing and notice you're not interested in it at all. Of course, you can always get out of the stock market, but this can also make you lose money if you decide to sell your stock too quickly!

Conclusion

No matter what age you are, you could always use some more money tips. The problem a lot of people have with managing money is they were never fully taught how to manage their money. For example, they might have learned how to pay bills, balance a checkbook, learn what a savings account is but they never fully learned how to actually manage their money. There is a lot of information which goes into managing money. This information can often be confusing to people, especially people who feel they aren't good with numbers. People are often turned off when they hear words such as investing and managing finances. However, one of the best ways to make sure you can live comfortably is through managing your finances correctly.

This book gave you seven chapters, each filled with their own tips to help you understand how to manage your money better. For example, you've learned some of the basics about managing your money, such as what a checking account is, what a savings account is, information about mortgages, and retirement plans. On top of this, you've learned that there are high-interest savings accounts you should look out for because these accounts will help you earn more interest than other savings accounts.

You've also learned information about borrowing money. For example, you've learned about things you want to look out for when you borrow money, especially if it's in the form of a credit card. You've learned that you can ruin your credit score when you borrow money if you don't make the repayments when you're supposed to make the repayments. On top of this, you've learned of a variety of different avenues you can take when you need to borrow money. Some examples are loans through banks, family, friends, and peer to peer lending groups. Of course, there are also tons of websites online that will help you in times when you need it the most. You've also learned the difference between a secured and unsecured loan. And, if you're interested in starting a small business, you've learned what a personal guarantee is.

This book also helped you learn a little information about debt. For example, I talked about how there is a form of good debt and there is a form of bad debt. It's okay to have a little bit of debt, but you want to make sure it's a form of good debt. Student loans, which are paid on time every month are often a form of good debt. We also talked about debt consolidation and how to pay back debt. Of course, I briefly touched on topics such as bankruptcy and how you want to make sure you if should file for bankruptcy before you actually file because you will have to deal with the consequences of bankruptcy.

On top of all this, we've also not only discussed ways you can manage your money but also ways you can make more money, even if you only have a little money to put in. You can still see your wealth grow with your few hundred to thousand dollars in many ways. We discussed a few online tools to help you manage your money. Of course, there are tons of other online tools and worksheets available. Sometimes you might want to try a few until you find the best ones for you. Just because you try a popular tool doesn't mean it will be the right tool for you. You need to find a tool that fits your style and what you're looking for.

Continuing on with our recap, you've read about ways you can change your thinking so you can better focus on managing your money. Sometimes, if we just change the way we think about money, how it's managed, and how it's valued, we will be able to manage our finances better. You've also learned that one of the best ways to manage your money is through establishing a budget, which you can do on your own through an Excel spreadsheet or find an online took or worksheet.

When you combine these seven tips, you're not only going to be able to understand money as a whole better, but you're going to be able to manage your money better. Through the seven chapters of this book, you've gained enough information that you can start to find your own budgets and ways to build your money management skills. Of course, if you're still in need of help, there are a lot of websites and money management books on Amazon that you can look through for more guidance. After all, just as the peer to peer lending groups state, we're all here to help one another. Just like the banks and credit unions, we don't want to see anyone fail because they have poor money management skills. We want to be able to help them grow their skills and become better at managing money. It takes time for everyone and you will need patience when you focus on improving your money management skills. Remember, it takes a while for old habits to die and, sometimes, in order to better manage our money, we need to change our habits and our thinking. But, with this said, it's also important to remember that you can change your habits and thinking with money, you can improve your money management skills, and you can see your wealth   grow.

Bibliography

Armstrong, T. (2018). What Is a Checking Account?. Retrieved from https://www.nerdwallet.com/blog/banking/what-is-a-checking-account/.

Armstrong, T. (2018). What Is a Savings Account? - NerdWallet. Retrieved from https://www.nerdwallet.com/blog/banking/savings-accounts-basics/.

Banton, C. (2019). Why Do Most of My Mortgage Payments Start Out as Interest?. Retrieved from https://www.investopedia.com/ask/answer/07/mortgagepayments.asp.

Basic Mortgage Payment Calculator. Retrieved from https://www.idfpr.com/FinLit101/Calculators/Basic_Mortgage_Payment.asp.

Basic Principles of all Mortgage Loans. (2019). Retrieved from https://www.leslierainey.com/basic-principles-of-all-mortgage-loans/.

Berry, A. (2019). Best Savings Accounts 2019: Best Online Savings Accounts | The Ascent.

Retrieved from https://www.fool.com/the-ascent/banks/best-savings-accounts/.

Burnette, M. (2018). Checking vs. Savings Accounts: The Difference & How to Choose. Retrieved from https://www.nerdwallet.com/blog/banking/checking-vs-savings/.

Burton, N. (2018). 8 Warning Signs You're Living Beyond Your Means. Retrieved from https://www.hermoney.com/invest/financial-planning/warning-signs-of-living-beyond-your-means/.

Caldwell, M. (2019). The Ins and Outs of Managing Your First Checking Account. Retrieved from https://www.thebalance.com/checking-accounts-2385969.

Chen, J. (2018). Guaranteed Investment (Interest) Certificate (GIC). Retrieved from https://www.investopedia.com/terms/g/gic.asp.

Dixon, A. (2018). Simple Interest vs. Compound Interest. Retrieved from https://smartasset.com/investing/difference-between-simple-and-compound-interest.

Elkins, K. (2017). 6 insights from self-made millionaires that will change the way you think about money. Retrieved from https://www.cnbc.com/2017/04/05/self-made-millionaire-insights-will-change-how-you-think-about-money.html.

Grant, M., & Nickolas, S. (2019). Compound Interest Versus Simple Interest. Retrieved from https://www.investopedia.com/ask/answers/042315/what-difference-between-compounding-interest-and-simple-interest.asp.

Gouge, R. 3 Practical Tips for Changing the Way You Think About Money. Retrieved from https://www.lifehack.org/articles/money/3-practical-tips-for-changing-the-way-you-think-about-money.html.

Government Benefits, Grants, and Loans | USAGov. Retrieved from https://www.usa.gov/benefits-grants-loans.

Hayes, M. (2019). How to Qualify for a Personal Loan: Are You a Good Candidate?. Retrieved from https://www.lendingtree.com/personal/personal-loan-are-you-a-good-candidate/.

Irby, L. (2019). 9 Tips to Successfully Negotiate With Debt Collectors. Retrieved from https://www.thebalance.com/negotiate-with-debt-collectors-4095357.

Irby, L. Freedom From Debt Starts with This One Thing: Can You Do It?. Retrieved from https://www.thebalance.com/ways-to-live-within-your-means-960044.

Josephson, A. (2018). The Dos and Don'ts of Borrowing Money. Retrieved from https://smartasset.com/personal-loans/the-dos-and-donts-of-borrowing-money.

Kagan, J. (2018). Personal Guarantee. Retrieved from https://www.investopedia.com/terms/p/personal-guarantee.asp.

Kiersz, A. (2019). Here's exactly how much more you'll save in a high-yield savings account versus a checking account. Retrieved from https://www.businessinsider.com/high-yield-savings-account-vs-checking-account-2019-2.

Kirkham, E. (2017). How to Manage Your Money: A Complete Beginner's Guide | Student Loan Hero. Retrieved from https://studentloanhero.com/featured/how-to-manage-your-money-ultimate-beginners-guide/.

Leeds, P. (2018). Here Is a Step-By-Step Guide How to Get Started Trading Penny Stocks. Retrieved from https://www.thebalance.com/penny-stocks-trading-guide-for-beginners-4123635.

Lowell, S. (2015). How to Control Your Debt and Improve Your Credit - NerdWallet. Retrieved from https://www.nerdwallet.com/blog/finance/how-to-control-your-debt-and-improve-your-credit/.

Make a Budget - Worksheet. Retrieved from https://www.consumer.gov/content/make-budget-worksheet.

Mercadante, K. (2019). 5 Ways To Start Investing With Little Money. Retrieved from https://www.moneyunder30.com/start-investing-with-little-money.

Martini, L. (2018). 14 Different Ways to Borrow Money Fast. Retrieved from https://blog.risecredit.com/14-different-ways-borrow-money-fast/.

Mears, T. (2019). 7 Retirement Accounts You Should Consider. Retrieved from https://money.usnews.com/money/retirement/articles/retirement-accounts-you-should-consider.

Mills, J. (2017). What are Some of the Different Ways to Borrow Money?. Retrieved from https://bizfluent.com/about-5076820-different-ways-borrow-money.html.

Morgan, K. (2018). How to increase your personal loan eligibility. Retrieved from https://www.finder.com/personal-loan-eligibility.

Mosowitz, D. (2018). Understanding Penny Stocks' Risks and Rewards. Retrieved from https://www.investopedia.com/updates/penny-stocks-risks-rewards/.

Mylor, L. Filing For Bankruptcy: 3 Most Important Things You Need To Know. Retrieved from https://www.forbes.com/sites/larrymyler/2017/10/03/filing-for-bankruptcy-3-most-important-things-you-need-to-know/#7924e70f7fe6.

Muller, C. (2018). Best Peer-To-Peer Lending Sites For Borrowers And Investors. Retrieved from https://www.moneyunder30.com/peer-to-peer-lending-sites-for-borrowers-and-investors.

O'Shea, A., & Schwahn, L. (2019). Best Budget Apps and Personal Finance Tools for 2019. Retrieved from https://www.nerdwallet.com/blog/finance/budgeting-saving-tools/.

O'Shea, B., & Schwahn, L. (2019). Budgeting 101: How to Create a Budget. Retrieved from https://www.nerdwallet.com/blog/finance/how-to-build-a-budget/.

Personal Finance News, Investing Advice, Business Forecasts-Kiplinger. Retrieved from https://www.kiplinger.com/tool/spending/T007 -S001-budgeting-worksheet-a-household- budget-for-today-a/index.php.

Personal Guarantee. (2019). Retrieved from https://www.investopedia.com/terms/p/person al-guarantee.asp.

Pritchard, J. (2019). Savings Account: Definition & How to Open One. Retrieved from https://www.thebalance.com/savings-accounts- 4073268.

The Risks Involved in Peer-to-Peer Lending. Retrieved from https://www.orcamoney.com/p2p-lending- risks/.
Twin, A. (2019). Guaranteed Investment Contract—GIC Guarantees Owner's Interest Payments. Retrieved from https://www.investopedia.com/terms/g/guarant eedinvestmentcontract.asp.

Types of Bank Accounts - What is a Savings & Checking Account l Wells Fargo. Retrieved from https://www.wellsfargo.com/financial- education/basic-finances/manage-money/options/bank-account-types/.

What Banks Look for When Reviewing a Loan Application. Retrieved from https://www.bizfilings.com/toolkit/research-topics/finance/business-finance/what-banks-look-for-when-reviewing-a-loan-application.

What's the Difference Between a Secured and Unsecured Loan?. Retrieved from https://www.onemainfinancial.com/resources/loan-basics/whats-the-difference-between-a-secured-and-unsecured-loan.

What Is the Difference Between Simple Interest vs. Compound Interest? -- The Motley Fool. (2018). Retrieved from https://www.fool.com/knowledge-center/simple-interest-vs-compound-interest-differences-a.aspx.

Winston, B. (2018). Retrieved from https://pocketsense.com/compound-interest-vs-simple-interest-differences-similarities-2229.html.

Yochim, D. (2019). Best Retirement Plans: Choose the Right Account for You. Retrieved from https://www.nerdwallet.com/blog/investing/best-retirement-plans-for-you/.

www.ingramcontent.com/pod-product-compliance
Lightning Source LLC
Chambersburg PA
CBHW060629210326
41520CB00010B/1533